Liv's Journey:

TRAUMA TO TRIUMPH

HOW MENTAL DRIVE RESULTED IN PHYSICAL RECOVERY.

Liv's Journey

Trauma to Triumph: How Mental Drive Led To Physical Recovery

Copyright © 2021 Olivia Gilling

All scripture references used in this book were taken from the Holy Bible, Common English Version and can be found at http://thebiblegateway.com.

ISBN: 978-1-7375096-4-6

10 9 8 7 6 5 4 3 2 1
Printed in the United States

Priceless Publishing®
Coral Springs, Fl
www.pricelesspublishing.co

Contents

Note of Thanks

I want to give a special thanks to my parents **Prince and Dorcas Gilling** for being there for me every single step of the way. You two have been a great tower of support and strength. Your loyalty and support are unmatched. Every day I wake and realize that God has divinely blessed me with His love and presence through the two of you. I couldn't have made it so far without your spiritual guidance. You are phenomenal parents and I pray God blesses you two for the hardworking, loving, caring individuals you are. I am so blessed and honored to be your daughter.

Special thanks to **J.P. Wilson**, who has never missed a day of visitation, no matter the distance, your love and support doesn't go unnoticed, and I love and appreciate you so much.

Special thanks to **Melissa Rivers** and **Krystal Benitez** for their display of true friendship and loyalty. You two spent the night at the hospital and made sure I was taken care of properly and that my every need was met. You are my forever sisters, who have been with me through prayer, laughter and tears. I appreciate you two so very much and I pray God blesses your every endeavor.

Special thanks to **Jonathan** and **Nekisha Barnes** who always went out of their way to make sure that I was well taken care of at all times, and showed their love and support through every phase of the process.

Special thank you to **the Gayle family** for the support and the push to accomplish this project and complete this book.

A special thank you to **the Baker family** for your genuine, authentic support — you are truly appreciated.

Special thank you to **Tracey Mattis** for your true love and support towards me, I appreciate you greatly.

Special thanks to **Anita Macy,** for being there for me every single step of the way, even until this very moment. You are such a pillar of support in every way, and my family and I are beyond blessed to have you in our lives! I'm so grateful for all you have done and sacrificed for me.

A special thank you to **Dr. Steven Lloyd Samuel Davis** for your incredible support. You are truly a blessing to the family more than you know.

Special thanks to my **Pastor, First Lady and Faith Tab family**, for all your prayers. You all are one of the most genuine church family I have ever come across. Your support and love shown throughout that hospital made every staff member know that I was not alone. I appreciate every single one of you.

Lastly, thank you to everyone who has been a part of my journey. I appreciate all of you!!

Chapter 1:
IN THE BEGINNING-MAMA'S DREAM

Jeremiah 1:5
*"Before I formed you in the womb, I knew you,
before you were born, I set you apart..."*

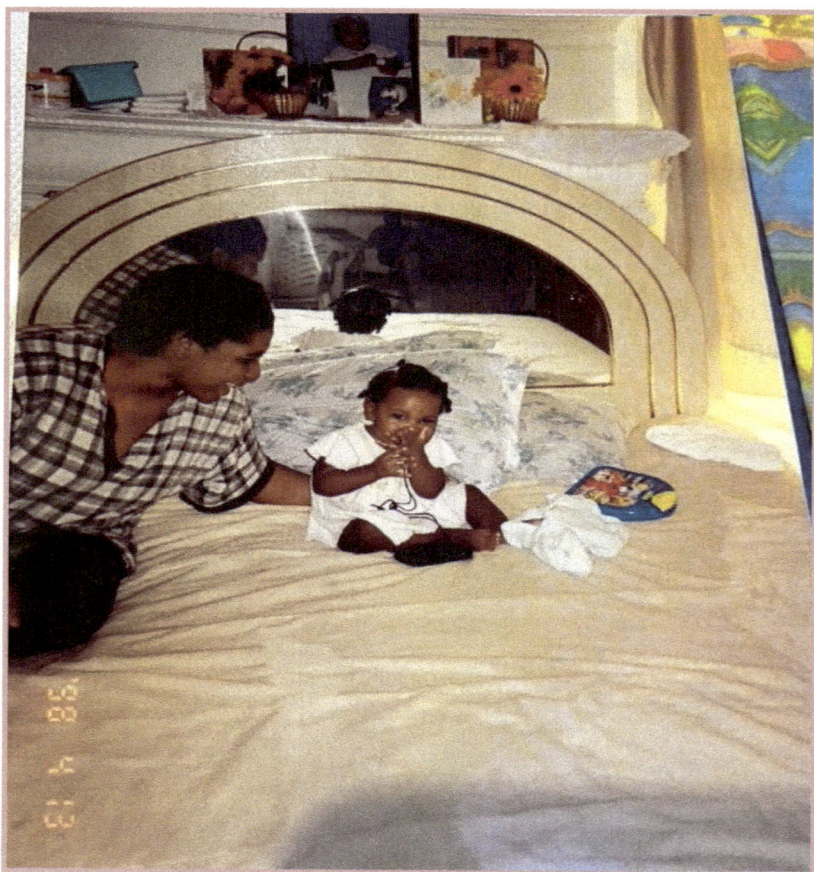

The label and characteristic traits of a fighter have been attached to me from before my birth. Let me explain. Before having me, my mother had a unique dream where she was standing in a river and all these little baby tadpoles kept attaching themselves to her feet. She began to brush them away, but there was one tadpole that would not come off and was fighting to stay attached. She shared her dream with her closest friend and it was then that her dream was interpreted and she realized she was pregnant with me. I was that tadpole that fought to stay attached. Liv's journey had begun.

During the pregnancy, it was discovered that I would be born with a severe medical condition — Sickle Cell Anemia. When doctors discovered this, they advised my mom to go through with an abortion so she could eliminate all the complications that would come with this condition before they began. My mom relayed the doctors' advice to my father. They were not willing to abandon hope especially, if the child was to be the daughter long desired. So with high hopes that it would be a girl, and a huge leap of faith in God, they decided to continue with the pregnancy, though the circumstances looked daunting.

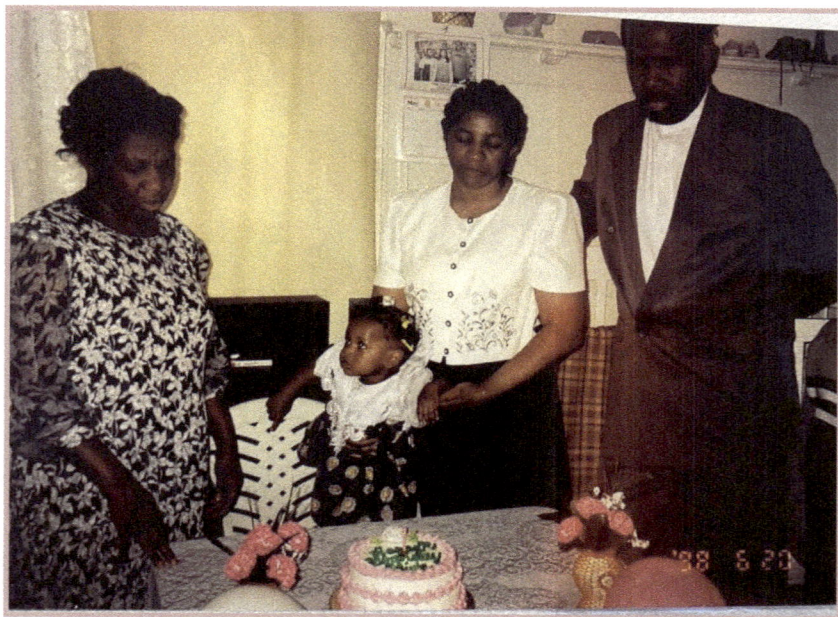

This is where the practice of faith in my life originated.

THE BACKSTORY

I was born in Brooklyn, New York where I lived until my family moved to Fort Lauderdale, Florida when I was 5 years old. In both places, I lived a relatively typical church kid life. In fact, my first steps were in church while my mom cleaned the sanctuary! My love for music also stemmed from this Christian foundation, as I grew up watching my father play the bass guitar. My identity as a worshipper was birthed within this context.

I grew up unaware of my condition, until I had my first *crisis*. A crisis in this context is a sickle cell episode, consisting of severe joint pain. I was 8 years old, at home laying in my parent's room, when suddenly I could not move and this excruciating pain came over my legs. I cried out and my parents immediately came running, and I was rushed to the hospital. The image of my father frantically running into the hospital lobby while carrying me in his arms is forever etched in my mind. I was admitted for a lengthy period of time, during which I also spent time in the ICU when my blood pressure and body temperature were high.

There were moments during this time in the hospital where my fate didn't look so promising, so at such a young age I realized the importance of a spiritual support system. Prayers were going up for me from around the world. In Florida, New York, the United Kingdom, Canada and Jamaica, people of God were at war on my behalf. I began to decline rapidly in the ICU, so they sanctioned my pastor and church family at that time, to come in and see me one last time.

THE PRACTICAL THING WAS TO SAY GOOD-BYE AND PREPARE FOR THE WORST BECAUSE OF HOW DREADFUL THINGS LOOKED.

But instead, they took that window of opportunity to intercede for me. A while after they prayed and left, I remember I was laying in the hospital bed, unable to walk since the time I was admitted, and I quietly said, *"I have to use the restroom"*. The nurses and my mother were getting ready to cater to me with a bedpan when I suddenly told them that I just wanted to walk to the restroom. The nurse, confused, proceeded to say, *"But you can't walk."* As if I didn't hear her, I rose up with her assistance, and began to walk to the bathroom. That was the beginning of God's healing power in that instance.

Experiencing and overcoming such trauma at that young age solidified my acknowledgment for God's existence in my life. It wasn't my parents' or my pastor's testimonies but my own personal experience that made Him become real to me. I was alive and grateful. How ironic that such a negative experience could bring such a product of gratitude out of me simply because those were the life-changing moments when I met the God who delivers — Jehovah Mephalti. God always makes His healing miracles evident for all to see and for all to know that He is present. One could ask, *"Why so much at such a young age, God?",* and the answer would be, *"ALL for His Glory!!!"*

One of my favorite encounters that Jesus has with his disciples is in John 9, when they stumbled upon a man who had been blind since birth. The questions began to ring, *"Well, why was he born blind? Is it because of his parent's sins?"*

Jesus simply answered, *"This happened so the power of God could be seen in him...".*

Initially when we think of living a life for Christ, we think of great paths of roses, sunshine and a bump-free road ahead. If we only understood that trials and oppositions we face aren't because we are cursed, or are being punished for some sins, but that they're simply an opportunity for the power and glory of God to be shown through us. Traumas we face are strategically authorized by God, for His miraculous hand to be shown. Little did I know, these set experiences would be needed to build my endurance for future encounters to come.

Chapter 2:
MY PLANS VS HIS PLANS

Jeremiah 29:11 NIV
"For I know the plans I have for you," declares the Lord,
"plans to prosper you and not to harm you,
plans to give you hope and a future."

The month of June in the year 2017 was a fresh start for me — literally. On June 1st of that year I graduated high school after being told I wouldn't be able to. It was a miracle in itself, that I not only graduated, but I graduated as the top student.

HOW AWESOME IS GOD? BEING A CHILD OF THE KING WHO HAS THE FINAL SAY, BUILT A DEEPLY ROOTED TRUST IN HIM AND HIS PLAN FOR MY LIFE.

I was the valedictorian!

Two weeks into the month, I was still on a high. I was excited for life, proud of my achievements, grateful to God and just bubbling over with joy. How could I know that all the plans that I had set for myself, — like going off to college and taking steps towards the career of midwifery that I wanted — would come to a sudden halt and be rearranged by His hand?

You ever hear the stories of when someone is about to meet into some misfortune or pass away, there are sudden special moments before the person passes, that can always be remembered by their loved ones? It could be something said by the person, a video they recorded, or even a hug that went longer than usual but it marks a special moment that would mark a significant remembrance before they left. I can remember having this strange feeling where while sitting in the car with my Dad at a store and recording a video of myself while waiting for my mom to exit, the thought of me passing away swiftly flashed through my mind. I was so afraid that I stopped recording immediately.

The exact day of the accident on our way to the field trip.

June 16th, 2017 was an exciting day that I had all planned out. Summer had just begun, and I was a camp counselor at my church's summer camp. Every Friday we would go on field trips, so that was the first thing on my agenda for that day. After the field trip, I was going to get the car from my mom, drive home and get ready, then meet up with some friends for a movie and dinner to celebrate our recent graduation.

I was anticipating an evening of fun and laughter with the people I love. And maybe after dinner, I would spend the rest of the night talking on the phone until morning, then sleep in on Saturday morning. My usual Saturday schedule just included thoughts and plans of my church outfit for service the next day and getting ready for an exciting time with my Faith Tab family. Plans, plans, plans...I had so many plans. In my head, the whole weekend was already scheduled and set.

But on Friday, June 16th, 2017 that naïve belief was rendered inaccurate when I once again was battling for my life.

I went to the summer camp in the morning and then it was time for me to pick up the car from my mom. My friend who was also a volunteer at the camp with me, took me to where my mom was and on our way there we were joyfully talking about the rest of the plans that I had for the rest of the day. I even invited him to join in, but he had prior engagements. As we arrived and I shut the car door while saying goodbye, that strange feeling of my own mortality came over me again.

When I was collecting the keys from my mom, a family friend who she was with caught sight of me and started to express how I was glowing. She kept repeating herself in an astonished fashion, and asked my mom if she didn't notice the glow on me. My mom and I looked at her confused and kind of brushed it off, and I went on about my day. I proceeded to drive home, get ready and started on the journey to meet my friends.

I was now five minutes away from the movie theater. I made a turn on to the road, and straightened up, I caught a flash of a white vehicle coming rapidly towards me from the opposite direction before the impact. It was an unlicensed 16-year-old driver with no insurance. He had just received his permit and was speeding on the road when he lost control of the car and T- boned me. What's peculiar is that the driver's side was the only side that was completely damaged.

THAT LIGHT THAT OUR FAMILY FRIEND SAW ON ME EARLIER THAT DAY WAS A SUPERNATURAL MESSAGE OR WARNING THAT I WAS SUPPOSED TO DIE.

The enemy aimed to kill me and that's when it was lights out for me and all my plans, and lights on for God to take over. In that direct moment, I later realized that there was a battle in the spiritual realm, for my life. Death wanted to take me captive, but being covered under the blood of Jesus, premature death would not be my fate.

As soon as the car hit me, I immediately became unconscious, which I call my God-ordained deep sleep. I'll explain more about that in a few, the EMT's came on the scene and cut me out of the car and as I was placed in the ambulance. God woke me up, allowing me to frantically tell them my name, my mom's number and that I had Sickle Cell right before I fell back into my *God ordained sleep*.

Keep in mind that all this happened while I was suffering from a skull fracture that stretched from one side of my head to the other side, which immediately resulted in traumatic brain damage. How could one in that state have a lucid moment to share such pertinent details? That was just the beginning of the supernatural miracles.

My friends that I was to meet up with, rushed to the scene where the accident took place and watched as I was being cut out of the car by the EMT's. As I was being rushed to the hospital, my friends and family were not initially made aware of where I was being taken to. My mom called every hospital in Broward County, Florida that you could think of. Low and behold, she called the pediatric unit at the hospital where I got treated for my sickle cell condition as a child, and God put her in contact with a nurse we were acquainted with who was able to locate me in that exact hospital.

As everyone was being alerted as to what happened and where I was, the plethora of faces started showing up. There were genuinely concerned faces and faces of people who I hadn't seen or heard from in years who all of a sudden remembered my existence because the worst-case scenario occurred. There were faces flowing with tears, shocked faces and blank faces.

I will pause here to discuss the first lesson I learned from the crash. As I laid there, I honestly remember taking note of the sheer audacity of individuals who now wanted to take pride and ownership in the title of *friend or family*. It made me realize how important it is to cherish and act in accordance with the true meaning in the title of *friend*.

A friend should be one who supports you through the good and the bad, one who stands on guard spiritually and otherwise when you're at your low point, one who sharpens you when you're running dull. Being a part of someone's support system does not have opening and closing hours like a coffee shop. Support from a true friend comes in the fantastic moments and the despairing ones, and there was a part of me that noticed individuals who were quick to run and try to support me in my lowest moment, but hadn't been there for any of the good moments in my life.

That is how God showed me the importance and the role of divine friendships and relationships especially in the worst times of your life.

GOD USED THE PRESENCE OF THE PEOPLE WHO WERE TEMPORARILY THERE TO SPECTATE AND GOSSIP, TO HIGHLIGHT TO ME THE FACES AND TRAITS OF THE PEOPLE WHO WERE SUPPOSED TO BE AROUND ME.

Those who will cry with me when I am in sorrow, rejoice with me when I am up, but will also stand guard and help me fight spiritually when I'm down.

There's a story in the Bible in Mark 2 where divine friendships led to a healing miracle for a paralyzed man. Word had spread that Jesus was in town and the paralyzed man, with the help of four friends, was carried to the house where Jesus was. Although it was full, these friends would not give up. They knew the power that Jesus had, and simply needed to get help for their paralyzed friend.

So, they labored by digging a hole through the roof, to lay their friend down, placing him directly at the feet of Jesus. Because of their faith alone that man was healed. I knew I needed people who could carry this dead weight of a burden and put me directly at the feet of Jesus. In this paralyzing situation where I couldn't do much, I would need those who were ordained to be around me to place me in front of the Lord for my healing.

A BATTLE IN THE REALMS OF THE SPIRIT

As everyone started to arrive at the hospital, I noticed that the Lord would wake me from my God-ordained sleep, have me say hello to each individual, call them by name, regardless of the length of time since I had seen them, and then I would go right back to sleep. The situation I describe here is not the medical norm for someone who is suffering from severe brain damage. The norm would be for such a person to be in a vegetative state.

My awesome pastor then arrived and glided into that hospital, ready to fight some spiritual battles. Due to my threatening condition, direct visitation was very restricted and limited, but he pulled out his chaplain badge and appealed to be let in. So said, so done. As a leader he made sure that he was in that room to pray down spiritual strongholds and fight the effective way to fight — through Christ. On the exact night that the accident occurred, my family, friends, and church family gathered in that emergency room and prayed.

The Bible says that we wrestle not against flesh and blood, but against principalities, powers, the rulers of the darkness of this world, and spiritual wickedness in high places. So, a war had already been going on in the spiritual before the accident occurred in the physical. The day before the accident took place, my mother had the most surreal spiritual encounter relating to the events that were about to take place.

As I mentioned earlier, I was working at our church's summer camp. Sometimes my mom would attend to assist. She did her morning devotional which included that exact scripture I just mentioned, Ephesians 6:12. There was a song that we were blasting that whole week called "Let Your Power Fall" by James Fortune and Zacardi Cortez, but as she sung it that particular day, a sense of mourning and sadness came over her.

The Holy Spirit then told her to prostrate before the altar and pray. As she got up to do just that, the church's doorbell rang as a parent had come to pick up their child. With that, the thought left my mother's mind. The Holy Spirit alerted her again and told her to ask the devil what he was up to as to why he was distracting her from praying. She says she looked in the corner and saw a demonic spirit standing there, so she began to pray.

She was led to take authority over the spirit of death, she then boldly said *"I take authority over the spirit of death. Olivia shall live and not die. She shall live to declare the works of the Lord!"*

The spirit then said to her, *"You can't take authority over death. Who are you to take authority over death?"*

My mother replied, *"I am the servant of the Most High God. The Lord has given me permission to take authority over the spirit of death and so I take charge over it now. Olivia shall live and not die!"*

As she said that last statement with authority, she said the spirit disappeared immediately. Simultaneously while this spiritual encounter was happening back at the church, I was getting lunch for all the employees at the camp, and as I was heading back to the church, I had this strange feeling of terror as I was driving back. I remember feeling anxious to get back inside, as if I was running from something trying to harm me. As soon as I parked the car, I got out and ran into the church and released a huge sigh of relief.

In spiritual warfare we don't always notice that the seemingly random burst of emotions that comes about, aligns with what's going on in the spiritual realm. The sadness that my mother felt while singing the song was an alert that something was supposed to tarnish me, and the feeling of fright was a notice in the spiritual realm that something wanted to harm me. If we're not on the alert when we feel these *random* feelings, situations can catch us unaware. Our spirit sends us messages through our emotions that we sometimes overlook because it may seem like just a human reaction or superstition.

SENSITIVITY TO THE SPIRIT, THAT IS, DISCERNMENT, IS A CRUCIAL TOOL IN OUR SPIRITUAL WALK. IT WARNS US OF IMPENDING DANGER AND CALLS US IN TO PRAY AND STAND GUARD.

In spiritual warfare, you're dealing with the master of deceit and lies. He will try and convince you that you hold no kind of power, or put us in a state of ignorance and doubt, where we think spiritual wars aren't occurring. If my mother was spiritually blind, she wouldn't have realized the enemy's tactics and plans, and my life would have ended if she did not stand and take authority over death in that moment.

Chapter 3:
COMING TO TERMS WITH MY NEW REALITY

As I was in the trauma unit, not knowing all that was taking place with my body in terms of injuries and surgeries that had taken place, I was constantly in and out of my God ordained sleep. I recall officially waking up out of it and seeing my friend Krystal and my mother in the room talking, and I then realized where I was and I asked if I was there because of my Sickle Cell, because that was the only reason I was ever in the hospital. With alertness, they said *"No, you were in an accident."*

As soon as those words came out of their mouths, the exact scene of the accident played out right before my eyes, like a movie. I then asked if it was a white car and they shouted, *"Yes!"* While processing all of this, I looked down and saw large, long, metal rods screwed into my hips in front of me, overlapping each other creating the shape of a triangle. Seeing that I asked frantically, *"Am I paralyzed?"* They replied that I was not, and explained that the rods were to help the broken bones in my pelvis heal, and explaining that I wouldn't be able to walk for a while.

As we were talking about this, I realized that I was using my hands to help me speak and that my speech wasn't clear. My whole face was paralyzed leaving me unable to show any kind of expression, communicate clearly, produce saliva, or tear drops. My skull was cracked from one side of my ear to the next side of my ear. I was hard of hearing, my vision was distorted because of the brain damage so I was seeing double, and also had to wear an eye patch over my eye. On top of all this, I contracted pneumonia while in the hospital.

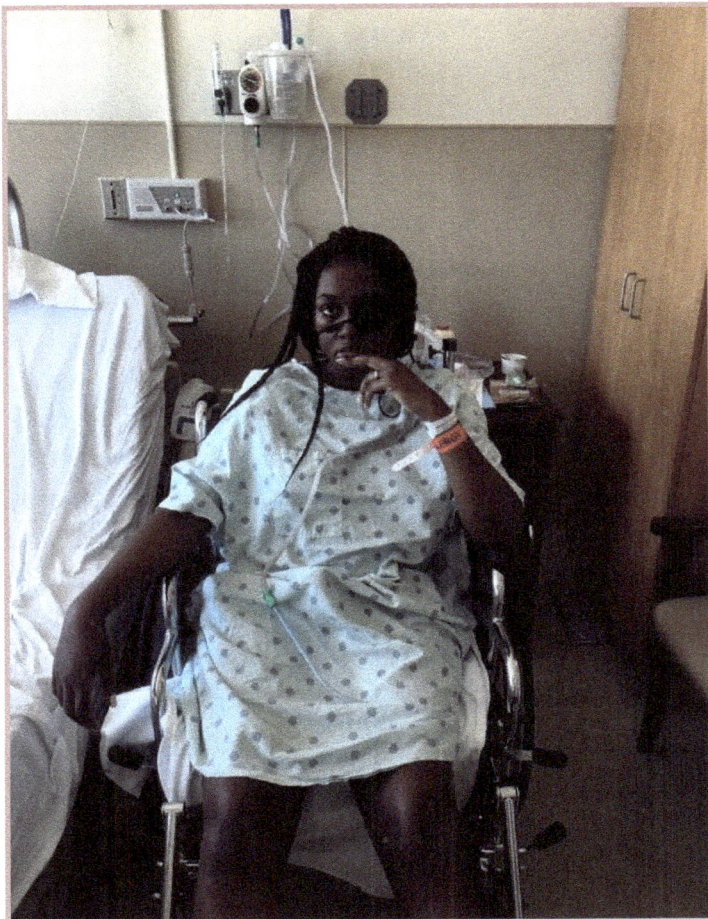

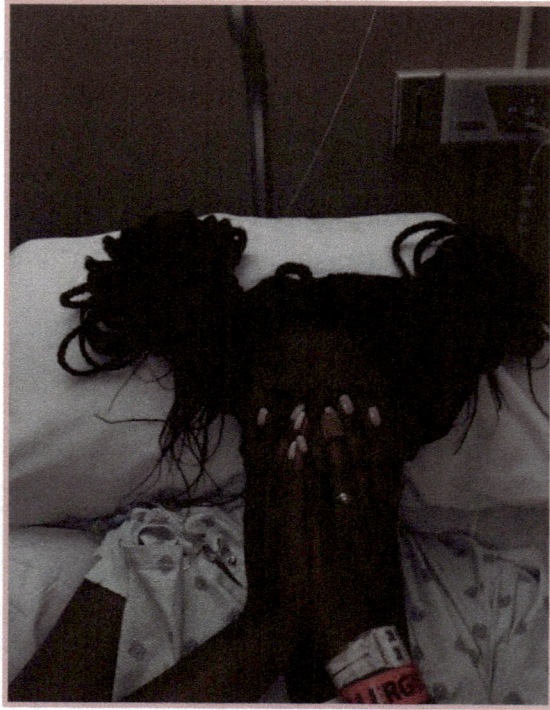

I always paint the picture for people by saying: imagine going to sleep being completely normal and healthy, then waking up with rods in your hips, a tube hanging out of your chest and your whole life's plans completely in question. It humbles you and makes clear that we truly have no power over our lives, and that serving The One who holds it, is absolutely vital. Laying in that bed, I had new-found appreciation of walking, seeing, and being generally independent. Who knew life could change drastically, so fast? I went from being a fresh 18-year-old high school grad, full of life and ready to take on adulthood, to being disabled, emotionally scarred and traumatized.

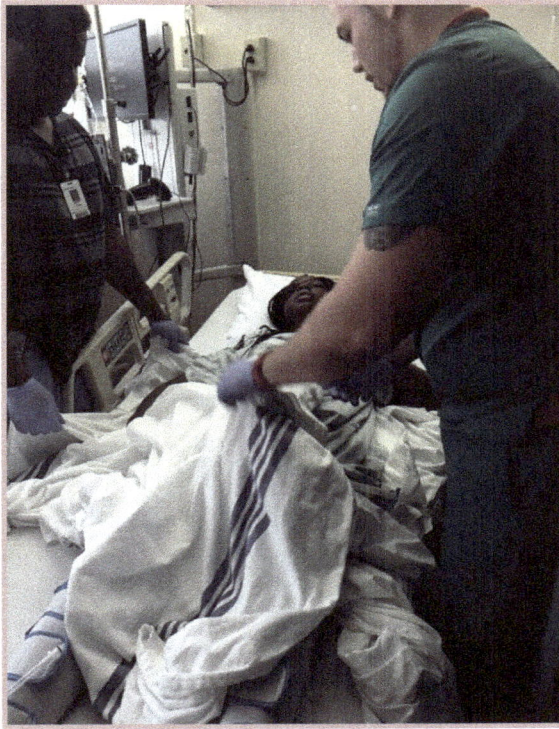

As the recovery process began, every waking moment was filled with emotions of frustration, confusion, hurt and sadness. Why was this happening to me? What did I do wrong? Why me? Why now? Day and night I pondered. I remember looking out the window for the first time since I had been admitted in the hospital and breaking down at the sight of the trees and the scenery, realizing how much I had taken for granted. The breakdowns weren't easy. I didn't know what to hope for. I didn't know what my purpose was. I didn't know why everything was crashing down around me. The list of unknowns was endless. I was hurt and angry with God. I couldn't comprehend it.

WAS THIS THE END FOR ME?

OR WAS IT ONLY THE BEGINNING?

This was the reset button for me — I had to start over. The day when I lost a great deal was also the day a new perspective, a new mindset, and a new me, was birthed. The girl everyone knew before was still there physically, but not mentally. Everything that was previously taken for granted, every petty argument, every little grudge, was all in the past. I was no longer that girl.

I now had something much greater to live for. To this very day, I get emotional thinking about the reaction of my friends and family who I knew genuinely cared about me. Hearing and seeing everyone's personal reaction gives me an overwhelming rush of emotions, due to the fact that my accident wasn't the kind of news that anyone would want to get a phone call about concerning their loved one. The genuine fright and concern that each person showed towards me moves me to tears.

One thing for sure is that I know that this situation wasn't only to build my personal faith and trust — it was also for those around me. I had to be the modern-day miraculous tool that God used to show His glory. Something we never really think through or put into perspective as Christians, is when we ask God to use us. We don't always know what Him using us may look like, but when making that request to the Lord, we have to take into consideration that whatever it is will cause Him to get the glory. This also means it will be affairs only He can fix, and those circumstances will always be difficult for the mere carnal mind to handle alone.

When we look at the miraculous Bible stories where Jesus did wonders, we realize that everyone one of those scenarios played out all for the glory of God to be shown. The worst had to take place so that God could show that He's the ultimate problem solver, especially in the problems that seems like they can't be salvaged. Take Lazarus for instance, Jesus had to let him die first for the miracle to take place.

In the end of it all, the witnesses experienced something they have never seen before and will now have a lasting impression of who Jesus is and what He is capable of. Similarly, here I was with this case that seemed dead, unrepairable and irredeemable. Many thought it would be the end for me, but I was determined to fight, and trust that it wasn't over even though my circumstance looked otherwise. This tragic incident was now for every person that ever crosses paths with me to see the true, redeemable, hand of the Most High God.

The reason why it is important to feed your mind, spirit, and soul the correct things is because that is holistically the foundation for your ticket to eternity. Whatever you feed, whether it be negativity, love, worship, hate or envy, your soul will reap those things. My mom will tell stories about when I was a little girl inside and outside of church, I would always worship, which is instilled in me until this day.

I remember when I was going to have my tonsils taken out at 13-years-old. It was my first surgery and I was completely petrified. I had been told stories before about things going wrong in surgery before and it completely shook me to my core. The Sunday before the surgery I begged for prayer at church, also the night before and the moment before they wheeled me to the operating room. After it was all done, they placed me in a room so the anesthesia could wear off. As I started to wake up, worship immediately came from my mouth. I was praising God for sending His angels to protect me and for bringing me through.

This brings me to the moments in the hospital while I was in my God ordained sleep. I didn't know what was going on around me in the physical, but when the Doctors stepped in the room with news about my condition, I somehow woke up and fixed my mouth to assure them that God was on the job. Even in my state of unawareness, I was still aware of the power of God and what He could do.

MY SPIRIT WAS TRAINED TO WORSHIP EVEN
WHEN MY MIND WASN'T PHYSICALLY THERE TO
COMPREHEND THE CIRCUMSTANCE.

BACK TO BASICS

On July 4th, 2017 I was directly transferred from the hospital to the inpatient rehab where they would teach me to live with my new reality of being disabled. While settling into the room, I remember looking out the window and watching the fireworks display, which was not my usual way to celebrate that holiday. Typically, the 4th of July celebration was characterized by the aroma of grilled hot dogs and burgers, while lying by the pool with friends and family to watch the fireworks. This point marks my lesson in true appreciation of the little things I had taken for granted in life.

The second day came around and it was like starting a new school. They had all kinds of physical therapists scheduled throughout the day to meet and prep me for my stay. Speech therapy, shock therapy, physical therapy — anything that correlated with my injuries had a therapist provided. They came in at precise time slots, like when it's time to switch classes in school.

On this specific day the first session was physical therapy. They came and taught my mother and I how to do daily tasks. They assisted me with getting out of bed and into the wheelchair, then moving me to the bathroom. As this was happening, I realized that as adults, something that never crosses our minds, understandably, is the potty training we receive as toddlers. Random, I know, however this action is taught to us with the intent to make sure we follow simple protocol for any time we feel the need to use the restroom, and to do so independently.

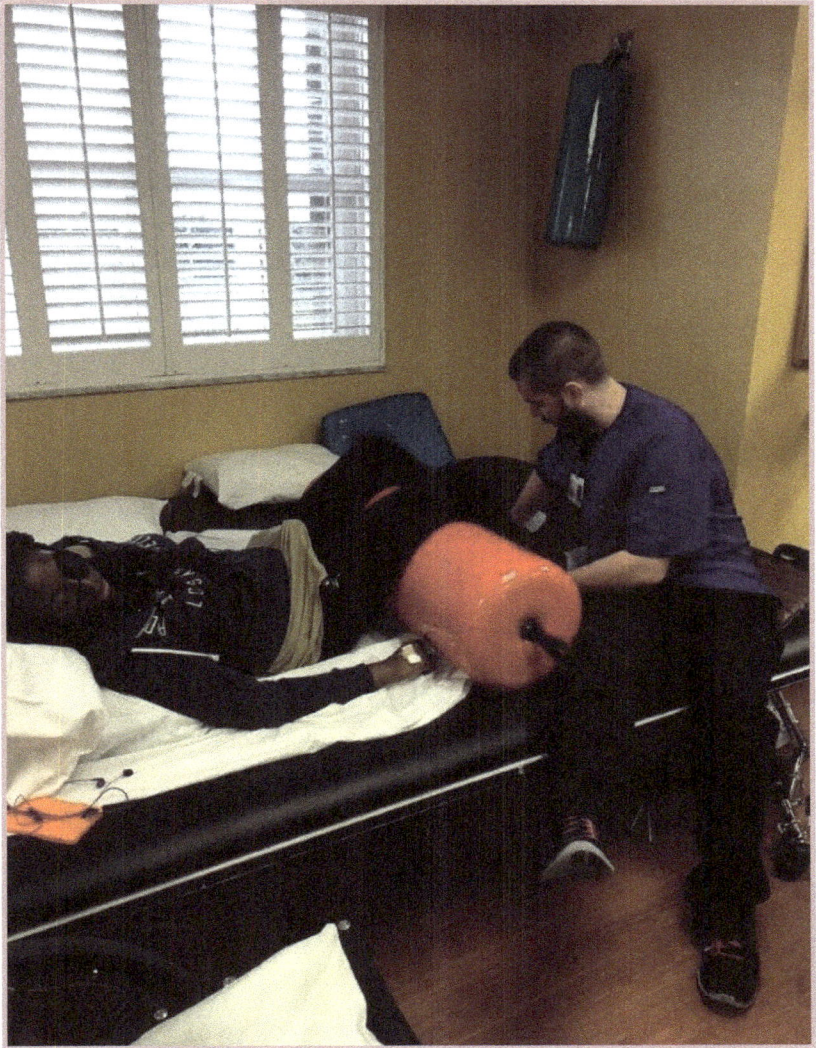

Strangely enough this was now a newly, yet peculiar discovered privilege that I no longer had. A very basic form of independency that I had once taken for granted was gone. With this unfamiliar change in routine that included a specific protocol, the appreciation of such simple things resonated with me on a deeper level. As the training continued, they assisted me in the shower, which was quite peculiar to maneuver, especially when you have large metal rods bolted into your hips while they also lay across your lap, like some sort of bionic human.

After the shower it was then time for me to wash my face and brush my teeth, and this was the first time I was getting a good glimpse of myself in the mirror and noting the physical change in my appearance. My face no longer had the ability to show whether I was happy or not. That warm smile that everyone knew was gone. The first thing people noticed when they greeted me, was now physically ruined.

As a young woman, physical appearance is one thing that I prioritized as integral to my identity. Beauty is something that we uphold especially in today's society, and I felt that mine was all gone. I no longer felt beautiful. I looked and felt like a completely different person. As I took note of every facial feature in the mirror, I completely broke down.

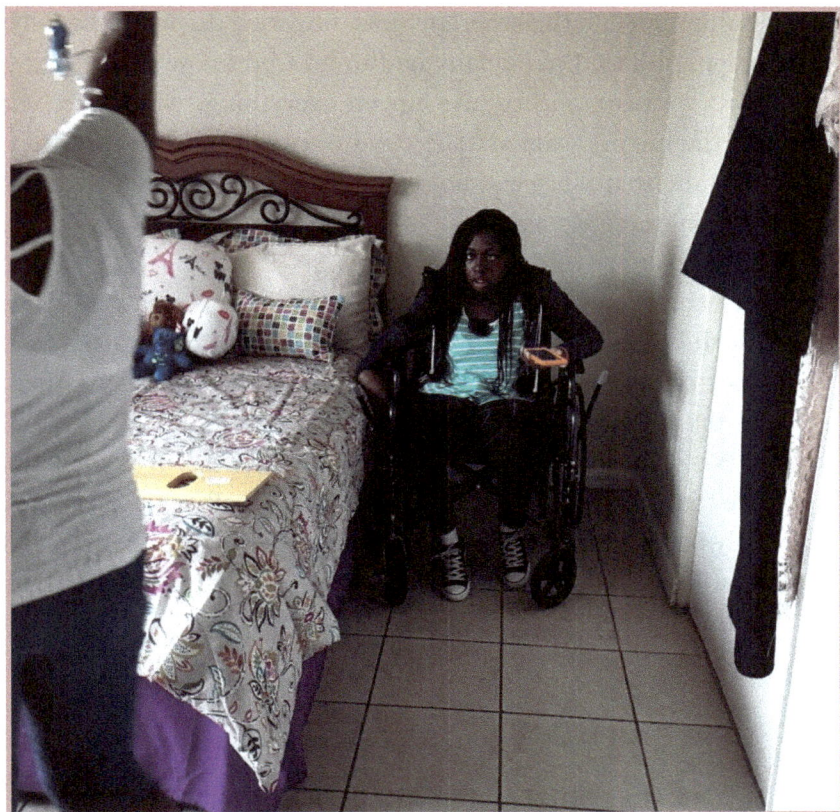

My mother stood behind my wheelchair trying to somewhat console me, as she too was this traumatized shattered factor in this case as well. This strong woman who I had always known as a woman of faith was also frustrated and confused and her faith was showing cracks. I then had the realest moment with God ever. In that exact moment as everything began to unfold and set in as my new reality, I had to pull faith out of the little hope I had left, but I knew it had to be worth something because at this point, I had nothing else to lose.

Although all this therapy was provided to help the physical problems I had, I personally had to let God know that it had to be Him or I was going to give up on everything, which was exactly what the enemy wanted. The devil wanted me to believe that this was it, and that there was no redemption, as if God was incapable of fixing a mess as big as this.

I expressed to God in that moment that He had to bring me through because a sense of disbelief and doubt had started to creep in, not only in me but also within my mother and my father. We were tired and weak believers who were fighting to stand strong on His Word in spite of the drastic circumstances. I needed God to prove that He was real. At that point in my walk with Christ, I could hardly believe that I was having such thoughts. Yet, in all this, there was still a part in me that just knew against all hope, that He wouldn't fail me.

MY SPIRIT WAS LOW BUT AS THE SCRIPTURE SAYS IN PSALM 37:24, I WAS NOT UTTERLY CAST DOWN, BECAUSE DEEP WITHIN I KNEW I WAS IN HIS HANDS.

The enemy aimed to have the reality of my current situation overwhelm my mind with just the views of all the troubles and negative diagnoses that were laid in front of me, trying to get me to accept the fate of what was the new practical reality of my life now.

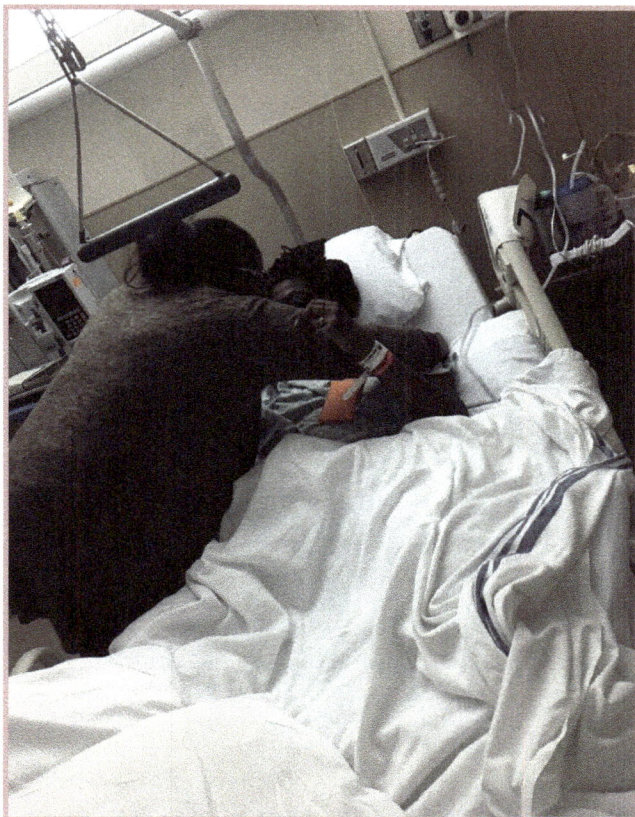

This brings me to the Bible story of Job. When everything was hitting him left and right, I'm sure he was confused on how such devastating events could take place so fast, and how everything could be taken away, especially when he served a God to whom he dedicated his trust and life to. I sat there breaking down and pouring out my heart in the purest form of authenticity, because I just knew this wasn't all that God had for my life. This wasn't the God that I knew. See the importance of genuinely knowing someone in any kind of relationship, is that you just know what they're capable of, their character traits, the pattern of their actions and their dependability.

I'd read the scriptures and heard the stories of how He brought many through. His word says that He is not a man that He should lie. It also says that He's the same God yesterday, today, and forevermore. In this case, I was expecting the God that raised Lazarus from the dead, that saved the three Hebrew boys from burning to ash in the furnace to come through for me. The same One who had healed my body miraculously at 8 years old when I was on my death bed, is the same exact God that would bring me through this dilemma because that was the God I knew — the God who can accomplish the impossible.

My tears dried up immediately and suddenly a peace and an ambience of confidence came over me. This encounter marked the moment I knew for a fact that things could not stay the same for me. I didn't know exactly how it was going to work out, but I just knew that God was going to show me His glory and I was determined to see it, but it could only work if I trusted His process, and oh what a process it would be!

Chapter 4:
GOD IS ALWAYS WORKING

Gen 2:21
*So the LORD God caused a deep sleep to fall upon
the man, and while he slept took one of his ribs
and closed up its place with flesh*

Winding down to the last days of my stay at the rehab, we had to practice how I would function at home with everything that I learned in handling my new reality. As we got back to my home, with the therapists from the rehab assisting us, it all hit me at once. This would be my first time returning home since I left the day of the accident, almost a month before. I left home able-bodied, excited, optimistic about life, and was returning a completely different person, traumatized, emotionally confused, discouraged, doubtful about life and my future.

HERE IS ANOTHER PIECE OF ADVICE; DO NOT TAKE IT FOR GRANTED WHEN YOU LEAVE YOUR HOME AND RETURN SAFELY IN ONE PIECE.

Entering my room with my graduation robe still hanging on the front of my closet, my diploma hanging on top of my mirror, and with all my latest achievements staring me in the face, all these flashbacks came to me with a range of despairing and defeating emotions.

Thoughts began to flood my mind. *"Would I ever be able to achieve anything again in a condition like this?"* I could hardly fathom that this was what my life had become. I was wheeled into my home by strangers because of my disability at the age of 18. A gut wrenching feeling of disappointment and defeat hit me like a ton of bricks, which strangely formed a deeper determination to get better.

I made up my mind that I could not settle in this state. As we got back to the rehab to prepare for my upcoming discharge, one of my doctor's came in to do an evaluation. As she was looking through my eye with her mini light, she asked me a simple, yet profound question, which would later reveal the strategic plan of God. She asked if I had been sleeping more than usual, and I replied *"Actually, yes, I have."* She explained that this was the body's way of healing the brain, so anytime we're sleeping, that's the brain's moment to start healing itself. I did not know the depth of that information just yet.

Suddenly, the true struggle of coming to terms with everything settled in. When you're all alone with no one watching, is when your true, uncensored, authentic sentiments are revealed, some that you didn't even know existed. The real test in this recovery was when it was just God, myself, my thoughts and my questions. No doctors, nurses, parents, friends or family...just me, behind closed doors, where I didn't have anyone to physically console or encourage me. All I had in those moments were my unrelenting curiosity, intense emotions, and the ears of God.

It is important that we prioritize spending alone time with God in order to hear and understand what He has to say. If we're constantly worrying and stressing about our trials, we won't identify the bigger picture and plan that He has in store. We usually desire that our problems be fixed expeditiously so we can go back to what we know as the norm of our lives, instead of comprehending the deeper meaning of a trial. For me, this was the atmosphere where I asked my questions and had real conversations, because I couldn't accept that this was what God wanted my life to be like. *This isn't what Your Word says about my life as Your child, so why?*

As time went on, where I would spend time in these private sessions with God, He revealed to me what He had been doing from the start of the whole ordeal. Remember my unconscious state or as I call it, my *God ordained sleep*? In Genesis 2:21, God put Adam in a deep sleep and performed surgery on him by removing his rib to create his wife, Eve. As I laid in bed staring at the ceiling, the comments from the doctor about my brain healing itself came back to me. God then showed me what He did with me the exact moment the car t-boned me.

When I was initially struck and unconscious, I only woke up at certain times to give specific detailed information that I shouldn't even remember with a brain injury as severe as mine. The case was so serious, that there was a chance of the neurosurgeon having to cut inside my skull to allow the swelling to go down, but miraculously it happened on its own quicker than expected.

GOD PUT ME IN A DEEP SLEEP SO HE COULD IMMEDIATELY START THE HEALING PROCESS ON MY BRAIN.

Every moment I woke up to address people who I haven't seen or spoken to in years, I did it with the recollection of their names and faces, which is medically impossible for someone with a skull as severely fractured as mine was. In the midst of danger and what seemed like my end, I was covered. Though I hadn't noticed it at the time, God had protected me and showed His might and omnipotence.

EVEN WHEN I COULDN'T SEE IT, HE WAS WORKING! EVEN WHEN I COULDN'T FEEL IT, HE WAS WORKING! HE NEVER STOPPED, HE NEVER STOPPED WORKING! HE IS THE WAYMAKER, MIRACLE WORKER, PROMISE KEEPER, LIGHT IN THE DARKNESS. THAT IS WHO GOD IS!
(THAT PRAISE BREAK WAS BROUGHT TO YOU COURTESY OF SINACH'S "WAYMAKER".)

With the knowledge of this, it created a drive in me to want and push for my healing. The Bible says that faith without works is dead. But how can we work for something like our healing? Of course, using wisdom and following medical protocols is a necessity. Those may include taking medications as prescribed, staying away from certain foods or following other doctor's orders on how to get better.

But when you add bold, audacious faith, with a dose of determination in the midst of all of that, your healing is undeniable. God loves to see our faith in him when things look impossible. It shows that we trust His supernatural power regardless of how complex the situation that is before our eyes, looks.

With my case I had a great deal of healing to go through, some seeming impossible according to doctors, but God already demonstrated that His hand was mightier than my injuries. Proverbs 18:21 tells us that life and death are in the power of our tongue, which means that great power comes with our words. Having received that revelation, I decided to use that exact weapon with my faith. I was determined to be healed.

In hard times, trials and tests, when our bodies are broken and our minds are weak, reading what happened over 2,000 years ago does not compare to our own modern day experience. Hardships provide an opportunity to see the Word of God come to life right before our eyes in our very own lives. These situations bring us to a point where we are forced to come to terms with our beliefs and knowledge of God. We get radical and desperate and start to pursue the God of miracles that we read and heard about.

If He is really God, can't He do for us what He has done for so many others before?

UNFORTUNATE CIRCUMSTANCES GIVE US AN OPPORTUNITY TO SEE THE SAME GOD ACT IN OUR OWN LIVES.

Within me grew a determination to see the omnipotent hand of God, that was mightier than the injuries that I had. I was ready to be healed and ready to give a testimony of the miraculous hand of God! With that fierce determination, I would wake up in the mornings and stare at the ceiling and repeatedly declare the words, *"By Your stripes, I am healed!"*

I began to believe that all the shattered bones in my pelvis, were mended. I began to believe that my eyesight was restored and the double vision would be gone. I began to believe that my ability to walk would return sooner than what was predicted. I began to believe that my face that was paralyzed would receive new sensations and that I would be able to once again close my eyes fully, make facial expressions, produce tears and saliva. I began to believe.

Chapter 5:
MANAGING TRAUMA AS A BELIEVER

Philippians 4:13

For I can do everything through Christ, who gives me strength.

Being back in the outside world while having to maneuver through it as a disabled person was one of the most peculiar perspectives ever. Being that I was in a wheelchair, I now had an essential need for different things that I didn't require before. For example, I needed the big stall that we see in public restrooms that we all prefer for better comfort, and the ramps to an entrance at public locations to just be able to enter. I remember always wanting to hide my face once I was in public because I was not used to being like this and it felt somewhat shameful. As if everywhere I went, pity from strangers and questions from people who knew me were immediately placed on me and I hated that feeling!

Going outside was one of the biggest things that I hated, and it also broke me inside. I was always involved in serving in ministry and I recall watching my church services online and crying every time because I couldn't be there to physically experience any of it. Church was literally like my second home. You could probably find me there even if we weren't having any services.

One specific Sunday I was watching service and began to break down and my mother stepped in and said *"that's enough, we're going to church."*

She said matter-of-factly, *"The enemy is holding this against you."*

I was extremely reluctant because I hated to be seen in that state but with Mom's confidence and support, I decided to go. She called our family friend Anita who helped to get me dressed, and they took me to church. As I was rolled in and was noticed, the body of Christ immediately flooded me with love, which released a feeling of contentment over me. I was no longer worrying about my appearance but I was more so focused on what the devil was trying to keep me from, which was my purpose for truly being there. As service ended, the guest preacher came over to me and decreed and declared healing over me.

During the drive home I suddenly felt sensation on the right side of my paralyzed face. With tears in my eyes, I frantically began telling my mom what just occurred. The Bible says *"one shall chase a thousand but two shall put ten thousand to flight"*, and as a believer I couldn't isolate myself with my trials because the people of God were set there to help push me closer towards my healing. After vividly noting this first sign of miraculous healing take place within my body, I was ready to fight through this trauma to get to my testimony of triumph.

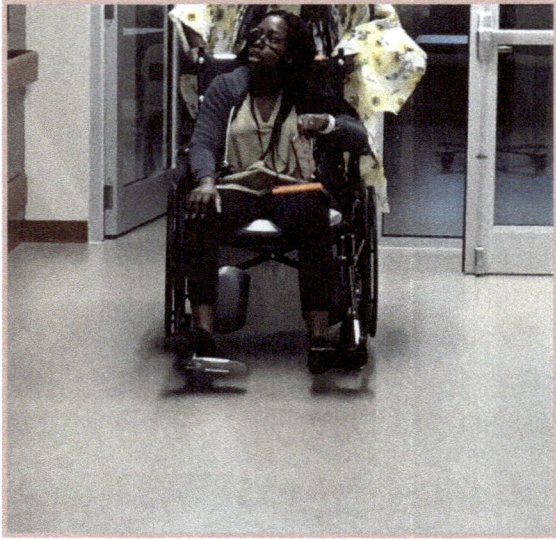

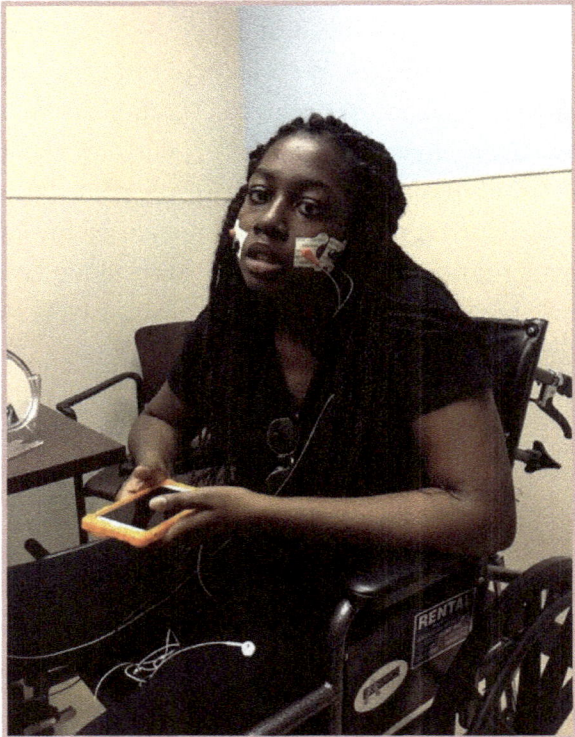

At nights, I started to intentionally go to sleep with healing scriptures playing in my room. They were the first words I would hear the moment my eyes opened to a new day. I attended each doctor appointment with anticipation and an expectation to receive good news. When good news didn't come as quickly as I wanted it to, it became a discouraging moment that sometimes blurred my vision of hope.

This circular process of expectation, disappointment, and faith to new expectation caused me to truly understand the real meaning of waiting on God. If I didn't comprehend this part of my journey in its entirety, then I would continuously put myself in a position of being disappointed because I wanted it to be done quickly and conveniently for me. In my mind it was about what I wanted, and when I wanted it and I lost sight of the bigger picture, which is that I was just a vessel being used for His glory. I forgot that I didn't get the option of choosing when my tribulation would be over.

There was one specific appointment one month after the accident, where I went in to check the rods in my hips to see if my pelvis was healed enough for me to attempt walking again. Although I was told this was to be expected in six months to a year, my faith was incredibly high, and when I got news that I wasn't quite ready it completely crushed me. I cried all the way back home.

When I got inside the house, I started to ask God a series of heated questions like, *"Why was the person who hit me allowed to return to their normal life without any repercussions, without any injuries and with no concern about my wellbeing?"* *"Why was he allowed to leave me like this and carry on with life as usual?"*

This kid didn't just cause damage to me physically, but he also caused my loved ones and I great heartache and emotional trauma that we will carry for the rest of our lives. And just like that, my great expectation was swallowed up by rage. My perspective shifted from the truth as outlined in God's word, to the facts as presented to me and the negative circumstances in the natural.

When we allow God to be in full control, it can be a difficult process that first requires our flesh and mind to be put into subjection. When God is working within the supernatural, his strategies and results are different from what our small mortal minds can expect. We live in a world of convenience where everything is on demand and at our fingertips, and we apply that same kind of thinking towards our spiritual lives.

MEASURING GOD WITH THE WORLD'S YARDSTICK WILL CAUSE US TO MISS OUT ON THE ESSENCE OF UNDERSTANDING HIS TIMING.

REMEMBER THE WAY HE DELIVERED YOU BEFORE

On June 1st just 2 months prior, when I graduated at the top of my class, that idea wouldn't have crossed anyone's, let alone my own, mind. My school's curriculum was part online and part in-person, but I was frequently absent from in person classes because I would get sick. Towards the end of my senior year, when I contracted one the most dangerous cases of walking pneumonia, I was treated in the hospital for about two weeks and then sent home on bedrest.

As I returned to school after recuperating, I recall going to talk to my guidance counselor and having her tell me point blank that I wasn't going to graduate. Ha! I took that information as an opportunity for the Most High God to show His might, and the greatest part about it is that it was not a challenge for Him. As she told me that, it was like something rose up on the inside of me because I knew who I was and whose I was. I returned home that day fell to my knees and spoke to God, and these were some of my exact words,

"God I am Your child. Your Word says that I am the head and NOT the tail. I dedicate my life to serving You and I belong to You, so You can't allow this to happen. I want to be number ONE."

When I finished my prayer, I rose up with a supernatural confidence that I couldn't even explain. The kind of confidence that made me look crazy for believing in the impossible to be done. The kind that left doubters confused. I spoke to my mom, who vouched for me that I would complete the work required for me to graduate. We spoke to the principal, who was a bit skeptical that I would finish the mountain of work in time.

I passed by the guidance counselor's office and reiterated with confidence that I will graduate. To my dismay, she replied matter-of-factly with two words that I can never forget, *"You can't."* Those words and her lack of belief in me stung but I was also emboldened. I looked at her and replied confidently, *"I can"*.

While I was working on the list of assignments, I put my faith to work and ordered my graduation cap, tassel, gown, diploma covering, and graduating T-shirt. As the days passed and I walked through the hallways, I felt the divine presence of God with me. His favor weighed so strongly on me and I felt it.

One specific morning, I was doing my schoolwork at the front of the school with a few of my friends, when we saw one of my favorite teachers, Mr. Jackson coming hastily towards us. As he approached us he looked at me and asked, *"Why didn't you tell me you had such a high GPA?"* My friends looked at me in shock! He then proceeded to tell me that I had a real chance to be the valedictorian. I jumped up, filled with excitement.

I could hardly believe I stood a chance. As he walked away to run his calculations, I immediately called my mom to tell her what was happening, and we began to shout on the phone. I saw my guidance counselor that same day and told her I heard that I have a chance of becoming valedictorian. She flat-out told me that it is not possible. At the time, the group of kids who were top choices of becoming valedictorian, were competing to see who would be on top. I was the last person to be on their radar as any kind of competition. It was clear that I was going to be the underdog.

While sitting in my English class, I saw Mr. Jackson coming towards the classroom. He walked by everyone and made his way to me at the front of the class. With a huge smile he looked at me and said, *"Congratulations, you are the class of 2017's valedictorian!"* I could not believe it! I got up and began to scream and gave Mr. Jackson the biggest hug. Number one!

Remember my prayer? I had asked to be number one and God did just that. With prayer, application, unshakeable faith, and a great work ethic, God placed me at the top. The group of smart kids I mentioned earlier who were candidates looked at me with utter confusion.

IN THAT MOMENT I LEARNED YOU DON'T NEED TO BE CHOSEN OR VALIDATED BY PEOPLE WHEN YOU'RE CHOSEN BY GOD.

When God has you and you remember what His promises are, you can never be defeated. No matter how complicated the situation is.

Just like that, I completed my coursework and started to get ready for graduation. I asked a friend help me with my graduation cap decoration idea. It was glittery and pink, with black rhinestone designs and a bejeweled cross in the middle. It had black glittery words saying, *"When they say you can't, Philippians 4:13"*. So even when they told me that I couldn't and I was the underdog, I stood up proud with my graduation cap that day, giving my speech of success while those who doubted and overlooked me cheered me on. Favor simply isn't fair.

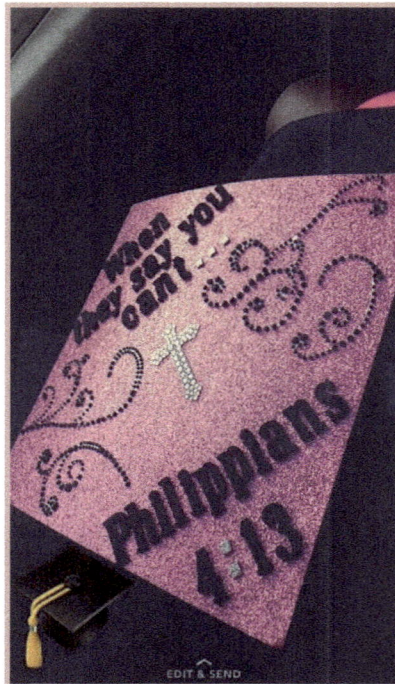

God's Favor Is Final

As time in my recovery process from the accident went on, every morning I woke up I would intentionally stare at the ceiling with hopes of discovering that my double vision was gone. On this specific morning I opened my eyes, blinked a couple of times, fixed my eyes on the ceiling and only had one line of vision! I made sure to look around to test my eyesight on different areas of the room to confirm that my eyesight was restored.

About two weeks after that I was scheduled for another appointment to check the healing of the bones in my pelvis. At this time it was only two months since the accident, and you'll recall that the doctors estimated that I had about 11 months until I would be able to walk with assistance. With that same mountain-moving faith that I applied when I was told I couldn't graduate, I was believing the same God who blew my mind then, to do it again. God gave me that victory to strengthen my faith in this situation.

Sometimes when people can't encourage you, it has to be the memory of your own testimonies that helps you remember how God brought you through in the past. When things seem impossible, remember what He did before and know that if you believe in His Word it is inevitable that He will come through for you again. Why am I so certain of this? Because God has been consistent through the ages. He cannot change and He does not lie.

As they rolled me to x-ray to check my pelvis, I laid there believing that those bones were mended. As I went back to the room, the doctor came in and scheduled to remove the rods two days later! It had only been two months...two months and my pelvic bones were healed! The day of the surgery came, and I remember going in and listening to the doctor explain how he was going to remove the rods and check to make sure that my hips were sturdy.

This freaked me out, but I didn't care. I was tired of being wheelchair bound. One thing we must do before we can receive our victory is we must be fed up with our present state. We must want and push for our victory and get out of the space of fear and complacency. We cannot overcome the circumstance if we have fully accepted it as our results or defeat the enemy if we comply with his narrative. I purposed in my mind that paralysis and disability were not going to be a part of my story any longer.

After the surgery was over, they placed me in a special room for a couple of hours to let the anesthesia wear off. As the anesthesia began to wear off, my mom handed me a blue dress to put on, since the rods were so large and stuck out, I could only wear certain things to cover them. I put the dress on, received my discharge papers and after two months of not being able to walk, I walked out of that hospital without any bondage.

I felt liberated walking through those hallways. It was as if I was walking into a new season with no chains holding me back, with more hope for the future. Two months after a major car accident where I was cut out of the vehicle, I was walking with no complications.

A week later I had an appointment with my neurosurgeon. At that appointment, questions were directed to my mom, to ascertain my memory of loved ones, and clarity. She answered each question but we were both confused. The neurosurgeon, with shock on his face, explained to us, that mine was an extremely severe crack stretching from ear to ear, and that I should still be in a coma-like, vegetative state, or even forgetful at least. He was staring at me in awe and examining me further, trying to satisfy the logical questions in his mind. He then exclaimed, *"Wow, God is real!"*.

If we knew the unseen of what God has actually brought us through, we would be baffled at how divinely protected we truly are. And so it was for each doctor's appointment that I attended afterwards. With each one the revelation of God's omnipotence was confirmed to me. Each one demonstrated to me that no matter how severe and complex our circumstance may seem, no diagnosis or verdict is more accurate or impactful than the Word of God.

The only words that can change your life are the words and promises from the mouth of God. From the beginning of my stay in that hospital, every negative word spoken from the mouth of a doctor was overturned by God's promise of healing and wellness to me. In every case, God provided a different outcome. Although it seemed like I was in the valley of death, I learned that it was merely a shadow, and that even in that place I was still protected. One of the fruits of the spirit is called long-suffering or forbearance. In striving to gain this specific fruit, we sometimes don't realize the process that comes with it.

In order for us to have strength to endure, we have to go through situations that make us weak so we can step into the realm of divine strength. The Bible says in 2 Corinthians 12:9 that God's strength is made perfect in our weakness. We are reassured in that passage that His grace IS sufficient for us. We must know what weakness feels like in order to truly differentiate and appreciate the strength of God when we finally receive it.

Chapter 6:
FEAR DOESN'T LIVE HERE ANYMORE

My first time being behind the wheel of a car again was a funny experience where God gave me no choice but to trust him. It was a dark evening, just some months after the accident, where being faced with a predicament, I had no choice but to drive. As I started driving, it started to rain heavily. I mean, it was pouring.

I chuckled on the inside because I heard God say, *"You have no choice but to trust me!"*

As I drove, I drove with a supernatural confidence that conquered every fear that tried to take residence in my mind. Since then, I've been back on the road with no fear. I just couldn't allow such fear to stop the progress in my life in any way, shape or form. That day I served Fear its eviction notice.

Today, I thank God that I look nothing like what I've been through. I never met or heard from the young man who hit me, or his family since the day of the accident, and with grace and forgiveness I continue to move on with life. When I tell this story, I make sure to use pictures and videos to show how far I have truly come, and the shock on the faces of people who hear my story is always priceless.

I am proof that God is still in the miracle-working business. People look at me and see a normal girl, who looks normal and put together, but when they see the visual aids of the trauma that I experienced, they cannot ignore the true handprint of God.

God did not bring me through such an extreme experience for me to keep it to myself, and not help someone who feels all hope is lost. I'm here to let you know that no matter how hard, severe or trying the situation may look in your life, when you have an immovable faith, a determination to see God's hands work, a willingness to fight, and most importantly life in your body, God will always see you through. No matter how long it takes.

There are times that I look down at my legs and become emotional because at one point I couldn't use them and I should have been laying in a casket. Yet, here I am, still alive and walking. It brings an extra dose of gratitude every single time.

There are so many supernatural aspects about this whole experience. Usually when a person endures a painful experience, they can describe how it felt because that excruciating pain is etched in their memory. One of the supernatural aspects of my story is that I don't remember the feeling of the pain from the accident at all! I can never take any of this for granted, because there are people who've been in this same predicament and haven't been as fortunate as myself. I know that without Christ I could have never made it this far. I owe Him everything that I have.

One thing we must realize is that God will bring us through struggles He knows we can endure. In the midst of Job's trials, he remained God's child. While going through his trial, I am sure he experienced confusion, hurt, anger and pain. But no matter how hard the situation got, and how gloomy it looked. God knew that Job would not curse Him.

When you're at our lowest and everyone's watching on the sidelines and wondering where God is, remember who your Father is. God will never abandon His children. Be encouraged — God will turn it completely around, then compensate and elevate us. How faithful is our God! He is so strategic when working His miracles, to show that no one else could achieve it but Him. He operates in such a supernatural manner that we cannot understand it. He is just a mind-blowing God.

Life will always bring numerous obstacles into your path. When it does, be sure to repeat God's promises back to Him, because His Word never returns to Him void. Those promises cannot fail whatsoever. God doesn't forget His promises. He just wants us to take comfort in them, and believe them. When we repeat it back to Him, it shows that we're trusting in his Word above all else. We serve a mighty God who is forever victorious, whose plans are to prosper us and not to harm us, so trust the process. Every step of a season comes together like a solved puzzle in the end, and then the masterpiece is revealed. We know that for us who love the Father, all things work together for our good.

God turned it all around for my good and now I have a testimony that will last me an eternity, of how the mighty hand of God restored me. I got a chance to witness His work firsthand in my body and life, and it has been such a blessing. Out of my mess and turmoil, greatness was birthed and now through His work in me, I am able to help and touch others. Since the day I was conceived, I can truly say it's been a miraculous journey and I know God is not through with me yet. He has turned my trauma into triumph! This is my journey — Liv's Journey and having been given this new lease on life, my journey continues!

Chapter 7:
THOSE WHO WITNESSED THE MIRACLE

PURPOSE CANNOT DIE

I was 31 years old, and had just come to America with the intention to accomplish my financial goals. My plan was to make as much money as I possibly could before going back home, But in the process of my money-making journey, Olivia decided to make her grand appearance (oops)! Thus, Liv's journey began.

Since the day Olivia was conceived she was a fighter. We fought together throughout my hard pregnancy and since the day she was born she became a leader and a worshipper. While every other kid was laying quietly in the nursery, my child was screaming at the top of her lungs. The nurse had to take her from the nursery and carry her to the room where I was and put her in bed with me. There she became a worshipper because the only sound she made there on was like a sound of gratitude and praise and, this has never changed. Growing up she was taught to put God first in everything that she does and everywhere that she goes, so she built a personal relationship with God that was unquestionable. I always knew she was destined for a great purpose.

The enemy knew that purpose was in progress so he did everything he could to kill her, his first attempt was at about 9 months old, and he lost! The second was when she was about 18 months old and he lost again. There were other attempts which were also futile, but the next major attempt was at the age of 8 but God showed up and took over and she left that ICU alive and kicking. The devil tried many times after that too but because of God's covering and protection Liv's journey continued. As I watched these cowardly assassination attempts on the life of my child, I realized more and more that she's the apple of God's eyes and that she was wonderfully and beautifully made for God's purpose.

I HAVE LEARNED OVER THE YEARS THERE IS NOTHING OR NO ONE THAT CAN KILL PURPOSE.

On June 16, 2017, Liv's journey was disrupted once more. She went on a field trip earlier that day with the children from our church summer camp where she had volunteered as a counselor, picked up her car and went home to get ready for a graduation celebration with her friends. She called me to let me know she was leaving home to meet up with the others.

It was the norm for her to call or text me to let me know she was okay whenever she gets to her destination but at about 3:45pm, I had not heard from her and I started getting worried in my spirit.

A spiritual visitation that I had a few days before flooded my entire being and I started calling her about 4:10pm and she wasn't answering. Minutes afterwards, I got that dreadful call and I collapsed to the ground.

In that same instance I felt the presence of Almighty God take over and start leading. When I got to the hospital it seemed as if I was dreaming, When I saw my baby I couldn't cry even though I was dying inside. It was in that instant that I decided I would have to trust God and act upon every Word that He had given me. My husband and I decided that the only way to get through this unexpected part of Liv's journey was to pray our way through and we did just that. However, there was a part of this journey that I didn't know if I would be able to endure, and it was my wheelchair-bound child who pulled me through. Olivia was the one that was speaking life into my spirit despite her situation and circumstance.

I distinctly remember a man telling me on June 15th, that she would live and not die, and this man's name is Jesus. He was in control since she was conceived. He was in control on the day she was born. He was in control at every attempted assassination and on the day of her accident, God was also in control and He still is. God has given this child a will power to overcome every and any obstacle, barrier or hurdle that the enemy has placed before her, and within 2 months she was out of the wheelchair and giving God all the glory. She has a passion for the gospel and has been a fighter, a worshipper and an overcomer since her conception. Here we are in the year 2021 and Liv's journey continues.

DORCAS GILLING – OLIVIA'S MOTHER

SHE BRINGS THE SUNSHINE

In April of 2015, I was a happily retired principal who had survived my service to thousands of public-school students in Broward County, Florida. Until a phone call came one day that unsettled my happy retirement.

"Hey, Vince, it's Donnie. I'm managing the opening of a charter high school in Margate and I'm told you would be a good fit as principal. Why don't you come in and talk to the people who are building the school?"

I wasn't sure anything in education was a good fit anymore. I had barely one year in retirement and was really enjoying the fact that my alarm clock only went off went it was my choice, and not by the demands of a job. But after discussions with my family, I decided to open Ascend Academy Charter High School in August 2015, and it was one of the best decisions of my life.

Why? Because of students like Olivia Gilling.

OLIVIA IS A RARE BREED AMONG YOUTH, WHO SEES SUNSHINE EVERYWHERE SHE GOES, EVEN ON A RAINY DAY.

And even on the rainiest days, she was always able to see bright sunshine in the future. She was so full of promise that she infected others with those rays of sunshine. Olivia is a doer among youth groups. Kids talk, they lament, they laugh, and they cry. But like many of us who passed through that stage on the road to happiness, they don't *do* much in their teens. They say they will, but it takes years before they grow and explore their world by doing things that make sense of their future.

Not Olivia.

She was working with other students at Ascend, she was planning her future with the support of her incredible mom and her other family members, but most importantly, she was doing all this while battling health issues that would have most of us hide away from the world, stay under the blankets, and let someone else do all the work. Even while feeling like a truckload of bricks was on her shoulder, she rallied, worked, and became our Valedictorian when she graduated.

Perseverance was her anointed name, and *Resilience* her best friend. I have seen thousands of students pass under my nose over thirty-one years, but I have never seen someone who strives for goodness, kindness, and intelligence like Olivia. I'm proud to be her principal, but I'm also proud to call her *friend*. When I think of all the reasons why I needed to come out of retirement and open up a high school, I know it a major one was because Olivia was waiting for the right school, at the right moment, to seize her future and make it work. And for that, I'm extremely grateful to have played a small part in her success.

VINCENT ALESSI – OLIVIA'S HIGH SCHOOL PRINCIPAL

THE UNBREAKABLE BOND OF SISTERS

Wow, where do I start? Well let me introduce myself. I'm Melissa Calixte. I am a 22-year-old Christ-follower, a full-time student at Southeastern University, and a bank teller. I'm technically Liv's best friend but really, I am more like her sister.

The first time I met Liv, was in the middle of our sophomore year in high school. We conversed and had a couple of laughs and from there no one was able to break our bond. Until I just didn't see her for a while at school. Every day I would always ask the students about here whereabouts, trying to find out if anyone had seen her, but no matter how often I asked, no one had seen the girl with the cheetah printed backpack.

Everyone simply said that they hadn't seen her. So, I waited... The day she came back to school I was so happy like a little kid when the ice cream truck rolls up. I remember that day we hugged for a long time. I asked her about her recent school absences and that is when she told me that she was sick. I was glad that she was okay.

Our sophomore year ended, junior year passed by and senior year hit. We were preparing to go into the real world with college, responsibilities and independence. As graduation slowly approached Liv was getting sick again, but being in the hospital surely didn't stop her from pursuing the goal of graduating. Next thing you know our school guidance counselor tells her that she won't be able to graduate. Yup, I know I'm thinking the same thing you're thinking. That made Liv work even harder. Trust and believe, the devil was attacking her but she didn't stop.

Now let me tell you all something — SHE MADE IT! And she was valedictorian, graduated at the top of the class. Isn't that something? Liv made it against all odds. I was mind blown. Something I've always seen in Liv is when she has a goal, she's going to accomplish it. She will not back down because she knows she can do all things through Christ.

We all went out to celebrate a couple of weeks after the graduation to celebrate. I was in the car with the rest of our friends and we were supposed to meet Liv there. I later get a call that there had been an accident.

In my head, I was thinking it was a minor little bump. Our friend Krystal drove us to the scene of the accident, and as we got closer to Liv's car, I lost it. Her car was wrecked. There was blood. I just kept wondering if she was dead. I feared the worst but inside of me I felt her soul was still with her and she was alive. We got the name of the hospital she had been taken to from the EMTs and went to pick up Liv's mom.

Later we found out that the EMTs gave us the wrong name, but luckily Liv's mom ended up finding the right hospital and we drove there as fast as we could. Her mom was in the back of the car praying and worshiping God through this whole ride. As we arrived, the nurses confirmed that Liv was there but we had to wait to see her. They put us in a family waiting room where Liv's church family was waiting as well.

As we waited, guilt came over me and I said to my husband Kendy, who was my boyfriend at the time, that I should've driven with her. Maybe if I was in the car nothing would have happened, right? He just held me and told me *"It is going to be okay."* I was pacing back and forth while getting impatient and angry because the doctors or nurses weren't saying anything.

I remember so clearly, the moment I stormed up to the tall Caucasian nurse who was sitting in the front and screamed at him saying, *"Do you guys know anything yet, I need to see her. What's going on! She's my best friend!"* Then I stormed out. Yeah, I know I shouldn't have but I did. I couldn't stand that everyone was just standing around.

I JUST WANTED TO SEE HER, SPEAK TO HER, SOMETHING... I JUST WANTED TO KNOW IF MY SISTER WAS OKAY.

Finally, the nurse came back up to us outside saying only two people can see Liv. Her mom picked me to go with her. I was nervous, my heart was beating fast. I just wanted to hear her voice. I see her and she's just laying down. All these things hooked up to her. I felt calmer that I was able to see her. The nurse told us the condition she was in, but I was just so focused on her mom's strength and faith in God as she looked at Liv.

When I went to sleep that night, Liv was constantly on my mind. Kendy woke me up and said that I was yelling her name in my sleep. That whole night I felt so worried knowing that my best friend was in the hospital. When she was sent to the ICU, it was mind-blowing because she was up speaking and laughing with us. Here's a little secret: every time someone came in the room, she pretended like she was sleeping. Doctors told her that she couldn't walk and healing would take up to a year. But Jehovah Rapha had other plans. He gave us a miracle!

All in all, Liv's journey has touched me. Many people would ask God why, but I know the answer. It is because He wants to show others that He is alive. He is still healing and still doing miracles. He is the same God that we read about in the Bible, and He will never change. This could have made Liv turn away from God, but she let Him use her even though she didn't understand the purpose, and that's what she is still doing today. God showed me through Liv's journey that there is a God who loves, and desires to have a relationship with us, and desires that we surrender all to him.

MELISSA RIVERS

OLIVIA 'LIV' GILLING – UNDAUNTED

We received the news of the accident and time stood still for a moment. In that moment our thoughts raced down memory lane to recall and recapture the Liv we knew, the Liv we loved, the Liv we could not believe was hit, harmed, hurt. *How bad was it? Why did it happen? What could we do? When could we see her?*

In that moment, memories served us well and we remembered a young, vibrant, energetic, conscientious teenager who was a shining example of dedication and leadership. We also saw her as fun-loving and outgoing. An exemplar to her peers, seniors and juniors alike. Liv was always at church gatherings. Not as a bystander, but as an active participant in any youth and young adult activity. You knew she was there because of her contribution to the cause, her infectious laugh and the roles she played.

When visitation was permitted, we showed up at the hospital, not quite sure of what to expect. What we saw, resulted in shock that was sometimes difficult to mask. Young, vibrant, active Liv was confined to her hospital bed and moreover, was unable to voluntarily coordinate simple facial functions. With no medical expertise, our only reaction was sadness. It was the most appropriate way to sympathize, while pondering the right thing to say or do.

SADNESS, HOWEVER, HAD NO ROOM IN LIV'S HOSPITAL QUARTERS.

She was always upbeat, giving thanks to God as she relived the events of the accident. We talked of her testimony when she recovered from the hospitalization, the pain and the recovery.

With talks of a long road to recovery, she made it seem like a trip that she would take in strides. Before we knew it, she was in rehab. Her body seemed to recover in record time and her mind even faster. At every step of the way, she spoke with thanksgiving, for her experience, progress and victory. Before we knew it, she was home.

We made visits to her home bringing peppered shrimp, which quickly became our *'Liv thing.'* Liv continued to give thanks as she recounted her recovery and her victories. There was never a dull moment in her presence and this made everyone confident of her progress. She spoke of her recovery as if it was inevitable and ordained to be so.

Her first day back to church was a day of jubilation. Her testimony brought tears to those who knew her story, and awe to those being introduced to the miracle. Whichever category you fell in, you just marveled at God's goodness and Liv's extraordinary optimism and resilience. She spoke of the near-death event as it was just a stop on her road to greatness.

During hospitalization and recovery, we sometimes spoke of her *telling her story* and encouraging others. That could easily mean just a testimony, but nothing about Liv is ever ordinary. She came back more determined than before to leave her mark among her peers and everyone else around her. She shares some of the effects of this tragic accident on her activities of daily living as though she has conquered all she could. Now she lives her life without complaint, without murmuring, without feeling sorry for herself.

Undaunted!

GLENFORD AND SHAUN GAYLE

WE CALLED IT A MIRACLE!

As we recall, the early afternoon of Friday, June 16th, 2017 was one filled with joy and excitement. We had just returned from the Truth Seekers Summer Camp field trip with little campers screaming which we took as a sign that they had truly enjoyed themselves. Olivia had accompanied us as a chaperone on the field trip. Upon returning to the church grounds at Oakland Park, she said her goodbyes and left.

Later that afternoon we got the call that Olivia was in a horrific car crash on Commercial Boulevard. This was quite shocking to us since she had been with us all day having her fair share of fun and excitement. A dark cloud came over the summer camp and all the excitement came to a halt. I told Donna about the phone call and hurriedly drove to the scene of the accident.

When I arrived on the scene, I could not believe my eyes! Before me was the mangled remains of what was once Olivia's green Kia. The car seemed as if it had been hit by a giant boulder. The driver's side was pushed in and I could identify everything inside the car just by looking at it. I must confess, I thought to myself, that Liv was gone! I looked at her car and thought there is no way she could have made it out alive. I mustered up the strength to take some pictures of what remained of the car.

It was then I noticed that one of the front wheels was missing. I questioned the gentleman who was cleaning the debris about the missing wheel. He pointed about 65 feet down the road to where it was. The force of the impact was so great that the wheel was severed from the car and rolled that distance. By this time the vehicle that had crashed into hers was already being pulled onto a wrecker. A feeling of doom and gloom came over me.

Why did this have to happen to Olivia?

WHEN DONNA AND I WERE ON OUR WAY TO VISIT OLIVIA IN THE HOSPITAL, WE ANTICIPATED SEEING HER IN EXCRUCIATING PAIN AND MAY NOT BE ABLE TO SPEAK WITH US. THIS COULD NOT BE FARTHER FROM THE TRUTH!

To our surprise, when we arrived at her hospital room, she was surrounded by a bunch of happy people as she laid in bed seemingly entertaining them. Olivia explained to us how screws were placed in her pelvic bones, she had spinal cord injuries, and her eyes were not stable. She had to hold her lower jaw in place from beneath her chin when she spoke, and her speech was slurred. Yet in all of this, she was still in high spirits!

Throughout her healing process, Olivia showed her herself to be a strong black woman. She was always thankful to her God and was confident that this too would pass. We all prayed, encouraged, and supported her as she gradually healed.

Today we see Olivia back on her feet again. She is the epitome of resilience and tenacity. By the grace of God, she lived. No wonder her close friends and associates call her Liv because that's what she does.

We called it a miracle!

LEROY & DONNA BAKER

www.ingramcontent.com/pod-product-compliance
Lightning Source LLC
Chambersburg PA
CBHW072209090426
42740CB00012B/2454